? Essential Question
How do animal characters change familiar stories?

The Prince Who Could Fly

by Philippa Werry

illustrated by
Caroline Hu

A Visitor

Characters:

PRINCESS, MAID, KING, QUEEN, PRINCE/CANARY, WISE WOMAN, NURSE

Scene: *Inside the castle, the* **PRINCESS** *is sitting at the window in her room, looking out. The* **MAID** *comes in.*

MAID: Good morning, Princess. Did you sleep well? Would you like some breakfast?

PRINCESS: No, thanks. I'm not very hungry.

MAID: (*walks over to window*) Here comes your father, the King, and his wife, the new Queen. I'll go downstairs and bring them up to you.

The **MAID** *goes out and returns with the* **KING** *and the* **QUEEN**.

KING: Good morning, dear daughter. You look pale and tired. Are you feeling okay?

QUEEN: (*frowning*) Don't be ridiculous! She looks fine!

PRINCESS: I'm all right, Father. I just wish I could come home with you.

KING: Well, perhaps one day—

QUEEN: (*interrupts*) Don't be selfish! You live in a lovely castle, you have plenty to eat—and still you complain.

PRINCESS: I don't mean to be selfish. It's just that sometimes I get so frustrated being stuck here in the middle of the forest. It's very lonely.

QUEEN: We visit you, and you're never alone. You have your maid to take care of you and to keep you company. How can you be lonely?

PRINCESS: It's boring staying inside all the time. I wish I could go out into the sunshine. All I ever do is sit here at the window and stare at the trees.

QUEEN: (*impatiently*) There's nothing to do out there, so why bother going out? Besides, you're safe in the castle.

KING: Yes, daughter. You must stay inside. It's dangerous in the woods. There are wolves and other wild animals.

PRINCESS: (*sighs*) I understand, Father.

QUEEN: What's wrong with you? Think of all the girls who would love to live in a castle without a care in the world. Don't let me hear you complaining again, or I'll be very annoyed.

KING: (*to the **QUEEN***) Maybe she could come home with us?

QUEEN: Certainly not! I don't like her attitude. She's going to stay right where she is. Can you believe she's complaining about living in a castle!

*The **KING** and the **QUEEN** leave. The **PRINCESS** sits down by the window again.*

MAID: Well, the Queen's sure in a cranky mood today!

*The **PRINCESS** sighs loudly.*

MAID: Her specialty is being mean. The King never should have married her after your mother died.

PRINCESS: I just wish she'd forget to lock the door after one of her visits. Then we could escape!

MAID: Well, at least she's gone for now. Here, take this cushion. If you're going to spend all day looking out the window, you might as well have something comfortable to lean against.

PRINCESS: You're always so kind to me. Thank you.

MAID: You deserve better. I'm going to make you something good to eat now. (*goes out*)

The **PRINCESS** *leans on the cushion, looking out. The* **PRINCE** *rides through the trees.*

PRINCE: (*pauses in front of the castle*) Hmmm ... I smell something cooking. Hello?

PRINCESS: (*calls through window*) Hello.

PRINCE: Hi. This castle has been empty for years. Do you live here now?

PRINCESS: Yes, I do.

PRINCE: Do you like horses? Come down, and I'll take you for a ride.

PRINCESS: I'd love to, but I'm not allowed to leave the castle.

PRINCE: Well, in that case, can I come in? I'm very thirsty and could use a drink.

PRINCESS: I'm sorry, but the door is locked, and only the Queen has a key.

MAID: (*comes back in with a tray of food*) Here's your lunch, Princess.

The **MAID** *hears the* **PRINCESS** *talking to the* **PRINCE**. *She puts the tray down and tiptoes away.*

The Special Book

Scene: *The* **PRINCESS** *is leaning on the cushion, looking out of the window again.*

MAID: Good morning, Princess. Did you sleep well? You're looking cheerful today.

PRINCESS: Yes, thank you. I'm hoping the Prince will come back today. (*hears the sound of hoof beats approaching*) Look, here he comes!

PRINCE: (*shouting*) Good morning!

PRINCESS: Good morning. It's a beautiful day. I wish I could go for a ride with you.

PRINCE: At least we can keep each other company.

The **PRINCE** *and the* **PRINCESS** *start talking. There is a soft knocking sound from another part of the castle.*

MAID: Do you hear that knocking sound?

The **PRINCE** *and the* **PRINCESS** *are busy talking and don't answer.*

7

MAID: I'll be right back. (*goes downstairs*) Hello? (*discovers someone tapping at small window*)

WISE WOMAN: I am the Wise Woman of the Forest.

MAID: (*opening window*) How can I help you?

WISE WOMAN: Actually, I'm here to help.

MAID: I don't understand.

WISE WOMAN: I want to help the Prince and the Princess.

MAID: How? Do you have a key to unlock the door?

WISE WOMAN: No, but I have a very special book. Take it and give it to the Princess.

MAID: What does it do?

WISE WOMAN: (*hands the book through the window*) Just tell her to turn the pages.

MAID: Do you mean she should read it?

WISE WOMAN: (*hobbles away, murmuring to herself*) Turn them this way, then turn them that.

MAID: (*to herself*) Turn them this way, then turn them that? What does she mean?

The **MAID** *goes back upstairs with the book.*

MAID: Excuse me, Princess, but a woman told me to give you this book.

PRINCESS: A book? But why? Should I read it?

MAID: She said you have to turn the pages. Turn them this way, then turn them that.

PRINCESS: (*takes book, opens it, and turns the pages forward*) Hmmm. Nothing happens. I feel a little foolish. (*looks out window*) Where did the Prince go? (*calls out the window*) Prince!

Just then a yellow canary flies in through the window.

MAID: Try turning the pages the other way, like the woman said.

*The **PRINCESS** turns the pages back, and the yellow canary turns into the **PRINCE**.*

PRINCE: (*standing next to the **PRINCESS***) Princess, here I am. What happened?

PRINCESS: (*touching book and smiling*) It's this special book. When I turned the pages, you turned into a bird and flew up here. Now we can spend time together.

PRINCE: That's wonderful! We don't have to shout at each other through the window anymore. I need to go home, but I'll come back as soon as I can.

MAID: Princess, turn the pages the other way.

*The **PRINCESS** turns the pages forward. The **PRINCE** turns into a yellow canary and flies down to the ground.*

MAID: Now the Prince is safely on the ground again. Turn the pages back.

*The **PRINCESS** turns the pages back, and the canary turns into the **PRINCE** again.*

PRINCE: Good-bye! I'll be back soon!

SCENE 3

A Cure

Scene: *The* **PRINCESS** *is sitting by the window smiling when the* **QUEEN** *arrives.*

QUEEN: (*suspiciously*) You're looking happy today. Why are you in such a good mood?

PRINCESS: It's just a beautiful day, Your Majesty.

QUEEN: (*looking closely at the* **PRINCESS**) Really?

PRINCESS: Yes, really. Don't you think so?

QUEEN: (*to herself*) Something strange is going on. Why is she staring out the window? (*to the* **PRINCESS**) Go and get me a drink.

PRINCESS: Yes, Your Majesty.

The **PRINCESS** *leaves.*

QUEEN: (*takes hairpins from her hair*) I'll stick these pins into the cushion. The Princess will get a nasty surprise when she leans on it. (*The* **PRINCESS** *comes back and hands the* **QUEEN** *a glass of water.*) I'm not thirsty anymore. I have to get back to your father. Good-bye.

The **QUEEN** *goes out, and the* **MAID** *comes in.*

PRINCESS: Has she gone?

MAID: Yes, and just in time. The Prince is here.

PRINCE: (*calling up to her window*) Princess?

PRINCESS: Hello. Wait—let me get the book.

The MAID hands her the book. The PRINCESS turns the pages forward. The PRINCE turns into a yellow canary. When he flies up to the window, he lands on the cushion and is hurt by the sharp pins sticking out of it.

MAID: The canary's hurt! Wait! He's flying back down to the ground. Turn the pages back.

The PRINCESS turns the pages back. The canary turns back into the PRINCE. He is hurt, but he gets on his horse and rides away.

PRINCESS: I must find him and make sure he's okay. But the door is locked, and the window is too high to jump from.

MAID: I know! We'll tear up the sheets on the bed and make a rope.

The **PRINCESS** *and the* **MAID** *tear the sheets into strips.*

MAID: Hold on tight, and I'll lower you down.

PRINCESS: But what about you? Imagine the commotion when the Queen finds I'm not here.

MAID: Don't worry about me. I'm looking forward to seeing the expression on her face when she discovers you're gone.

The **MAID** *lowers the* **PRINCESS** *down.*

PRINCESS: There! I made it!

MAID: (*calls out the window*) Now go and find the Prince. Quickly!

PRINCESS: But I don't know which way to go.

The **WISE WOMAN** *comes out of the forest. She approaches the* **PRINCESS***.*

WISE WOMAN: Just follow the river. And take this. (*hands her some ointment*) The Prince is badly hurt, but this will save him.

PRINCESS: Thank you!

The **PRINCESS** *takes off, running through the forest holding the ointment.*

PRINCESS: (*to herself*) I wonder if the Prince will recognize me?

The **PRINCESS** *arrives at the palace. A* **NURSE** *leads her to the* **PRINCE**, *who is asleep.*

PRINCESS: We need to use the Wise Woman's ointment to cure him.

The **PRINCESS** *gives the ointment to the nurse, who rubs it into his wounds. The* **PRINCE** *slowly opens his eyes.*

PRINCESS: Hello, Prince. Do you know who I am?

PRINCE: Of course. You are as familiar to me as my own heart. How did you get here?

PRINCESS: I just followed the river ... and my heart led me the rest of the way.

Respond to Reading

Summarize

Use details from *The Prince Who Could Fly* to summarize the selection. Your graphic organizer may help you.

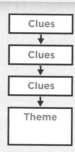

Text Evidence

1. What text features help you identify this as a drama? GENRE

2. How does the prince help the princess? THEME

3. What does the word *dangerous* mean on page 3? Use context clues to define the word. What antonym for *dangerous* helped you figure out its meaning? SYNONYMS AND ANTONYMS

4. Write about the message the author communicates by having the princess go to help the prince. WRITE ABOUT READING

Compare Texts

Read a story about an animal who solves a mystery.

The Mystery of the Spotted Dogs

"Mrs. Marjoram," the animals said. "Where are you going?"

"I've just seen an advertisement in the newspaper," said Mrs. Marjoram. "'Genuine Dalmatian puppies for sale, good price.'"

At first, Detective Dog didn't hear. Then he was woken from a pleasant dream by Duck's quacking. "What's happening?" asked Detective Dog.

"Mrs. Marjoram wants a Dalmatian puppy," said Tabitha Cat.

Mrs. Marjoram told Detective Dog the price.

"That's *very* expensive," said Detective Dog. "I think I'd better come along."

"Can we come, too?" asked all the animals.

"Not all of you," said Detective Dog, but Sheep, Goose, Duck, Pig, and Cat all squeezed in the back of the car anyway.

After a short drive, they arrived at a farm.

Mrs. Marjoram knocked on the door. A man opened it and peered out at them.

"We've come to look at your puppies," said Mrs. Marjoram.

"Come this way," the man replied.

He took them out to the barn. "Here they are. You're lucky I haven't sold them yet. People have been calling all day."

"Aren't they cute!" said Goose.

"So little! So spotty!" said Pig.

"How old are they?" Detective Dog asked the man.

Illustration: David Opie

"Only a few days old," said the owner.

"Are they genuine Dalmatian puppies?" asked Detective Dog.

"Yes," the man replied. "See their spots?"

"What do you think?" Mrs. Marjoram whispered to Detective Dog.

"Mrs. Marjoram, these are very cute puppies, but they aren't genuine Dalmatians. So I'd advise you not to buy one."

"How do you know they aren't genuine Dalmatians?" asked Mrs. Marjoram, looking at the puppies tumbling about in their pen.

"These puppies are only a few days old, and they already have spots," said Detective Dog. "Dalmatian puppies are born without spots. These spots are painted on!"

"Detective Dog, you are so smart. I'm glad you came with me today," said Mrs. Marjoram.

Make Connections

How does Detective Dog help Mrs. Marjoram?
ESSENTIAL QUESTION

How is the Wise Woman's role in *The Prince Who Could Fly* similar to that of Detective Dog in *The Mystery of the Spotted Dogs?* TEXT TO TEXT

Focus on Genre

Dramas Dramas are stories that are performed for an audience. The text is mostly dialogue, and there are stage directions that describe what the characters do. Dramas have scenes instead of chapters.

Read and Find In *The Prince Who Could Fly*, the stage directions are in italics. They tell the actors where the scene is set and what the characters should do. The name of the speaker comes first, and a colon separates the name of the character from the words the character speaks.

Your Turn

Turn to page 6. Find the stage directions that tell each character what to do.

Turn to page 15. Write a short scene that shows how the Queen reacts when she discovers the Princess is gone. Remember to use the drama text features to show who is speaking and what each character does.